Katarzyna Biedrzycka

While every precaution has been taken in the preparation of this book, the publisher assumes no responsibility for errors or omissions, or for damages resulting from the use of the information contained herein.

MENTAL LANDSCAPES - PRACTICAL GUIDE TO EFFECTIVE AFFIRMATIONS FOR BEGINNERS

First edition. February 11, 2024.

Copyright © 2024 Katarzyna Biedrzycka.

ISBN: 979-8224525768

Written by Katarzyna Biedrzycka.

Also by Katarzyna Biedrzycka

Huna
Huna - Discovering the Path to Your Silence

Mental Landscapes
Mental Landscapes - Practical Guide to Effective Meditation for Beginners
Mental Landscapes - Practical Guide to Effective Affirmations for Beginners

Mental Landscapes

Practical Guide to Effective Affirmations for Beginners

Preface

Welcome, Dear Reader.

Have you ever recited affirmations hoping for positive changes, only to be met with a wave of disappointment instead? Perhaps you repeated every morning, "I will be happy when I achieve success," but instead of feeling empowered, you felt only more frustration, seeing no real results. This book is the answer to those challenges. Here, I unveil the most common mistakes that can sabotage your affirmation practices, and explain why they are so crucial.

One of the key aspects that I focus on in this book is the importance of aligning affirmations with the current emotional state of the person using them. It's not just a matter of choosing the right words, but also understanding and accepting your own feelings. An affirmation that is incongruent with your current emotional experience can seem ineffective or even provoke resistance. Therefore, it is important to learn how to select affirmations that resonate with your inner world and support you on the way to achieving your goals.

I will present studies that you can analyze to understand the ideas contained here more deeply. However, most importantly, we will walk together on the path of creating and implementing effective affirmations that have the power to transform your world.

Another essential tool you will find in this book is a monthly journal of effective affirmations. Its purpose is to help you develop the habit of working with affirmations daily. This journal provides a space where you can record your progress, reflections, and feelings, which is invaluable help in solidifying new, positive patterns of thinking. I encourage you to use this journal regularly, as consistency in applying affirmations is key to their effectiveness. Systematically recording your experiences and progress will allow a better understanding of your inner journey and observe how your life changes through the consistent application of affirmations.

I will share knowledge and experience gathered over the years, showing how properly formulated affirmations can become a powerful tool for positive change. You will discover not only the theoretical foundations but, most importantly, practical methods and exercises. They are the key to breaking negative thought patterns and replacing them with constructive beliefs.

The stories of people who have transformed their daily lives through affirmations are not only inspiring but also testify to the universality of this technique. It's a pragmatic approach that brings tangible results.

In this book, you will also find comprehensive exercises for creating your affirmations. We will analyze the effectiveness of selected formulations and sentence structures, tailoring them to your unique needs and aspirations.

I assure you that mastering the art of creating personalized affirmations in the right way will open the door to transformation and shaping reality according to your desires. It's a journey full of discoveries, during which you will learn how to use the power of your own thoughts and words to create the life you expect. I invite you to this transformative journey, offering not only knowledge but tools for creating the life you dream of. Let's start it together.

Who is this book for?

This book is written with a broad spectrum of individuals in mind who wish to introduce positive changes into their lives through affirmations. It is perfect for anyone looking for inspiration and practical tools for personal development.

— **For beginners in the field of affirmations:** Individuals just starting their journey with affirmations, aiming to understand how to apply them correctly, will find an accessible guide here. This guide will help them avoid common mistakes and effectively incorporate affirmations into their daily practice.

— **For those who have previously experienced failures with affirmations:** For people who have already tried using affirmations but without satisfactory results, this book offers new perspectives and methods. It helps understand the reasons behind past failures and shows how to overcome them.

— **For individuals seeking personal development:** If someone is interested in deeper self-awareness and wants to work on their self-esteem, motivation, or achieving personal goals, they will find plenty of valuable advice and exercises here.

— **For professionals in coaching and psychology:** Coaches, psychologists, and other professionals can use this book as an additional source of inspiration and knowledge to support their clients in the process of change and achieving their goals.

— **For anyone looking to improve the quality of their life:** Regardless of whether someone wants to enhance their relationships, career, health, or simply seeks a way to increase their overall sense of happiness and fulfillment, this book offers tools that can assist in these endeavors.

In short, this book is for anyone who wants to actively work on their life, using the power of affirmations to create positive changes and achieve personal goals. No matter where you currently are on your life's journey, this book has the potential to become a valuable source of knowledge and inspiration.

Chapter 1 — What Are Affirmations?

Definition and Significance of Affirmations

Affirmations are positive statements used to bring about change in our way of thinking and acting. They are self-help tools utilized for building self-confidence, motivation, and a positive outlook on life. Affirmations work through the repetition of positive statements that gradually replace negative thoughts and beliefs. In this way, they help break down barriers on the path to achieving goals and dreams. Their impact on our beliefs and attitudes translates into daily actions and decisions.

It's important to emphasize that the effectiveness of affirmations depends on their content, as well as the regularity and manner of their application. Ideally, they should be personalized and match the individual needs and goals of the person using them, formulated in the present tense to evoke a sense of positive changes occurring here and now. In the subsequent chapters of this book, we will present specific examples of affirmations and discuss common pitfalls and mistakes associated with their improper use.

It is also crucial to understand that affirmations are not a magical solution to all problems. They are rather a tool supporting the process of personal development, which requires time, patience, and consistency in action. For affirmations to be effective, they should be part of a broader personal development plan, including activities such as goal setting, habit work, or coaching. Affirmations can only be effective when accompanied by actions aimed at achieving set goals. They also play a significant role in overcoming emotional blocks, bad habits, and low self-esteem. By regularly repeating positive statements like, "I am strong and capable of overcoming difficulties," one can change the way they think about themselves and their capabilities. They help in building a positive internal dialogue, which is key in breaking negative beliefs and strengthening self-esteem.

Emphasizing the regularity of practicing affirmations is essential. It is not the isolated repetitions, but the continuous practice that is the key to success. It's also worth being aware of potential challenges, such as initial doubts or difficulties in maintaining regularity, which may arise on the path to achieving desired changes.

Through affirmations, it is also possible to effectively change bad habits, replacing negative thinking patterns with constructive beliefs. In this way, affirmations become a tool supporting both emotional and behavioral personal development.

The Significance of Affirmations in Personal Development

Affirmations in personal development play a crucial role. They become a tool enabling profound transformation in thinking and acting, allowing individuals to achieve their goals and dreams. In the personal development process, affirmations act like an anchor, maintaining course towards desired changes and aspirations.

By using affirmations, one can effectively influence their beliefs and the way they perceive themselves and their surroundings. This is the foundation of building a better life. Affirmations can be used to strengthen positive thinking, especially important in difficult situations. They help break negative thinking patterns, replacing them with more productive and positive beliefs.

This, in turn, leads to better stress management. Affirmations support the development of greater emotional resilience. They teach how to manage emotions in the face of challenges, instead of letting them control us. For example, the affirmation "I can find peace even in difficult situations" helps strengthen mental resilience. As a result, people who use such affirmations often feel less pressure and more control over their emotional reactions.

Thus, affirmations become a powerful tool in the arsenal of anyone striving for personal development and increasing their mental resilience. They enable not only the achievement of specific goals but also the building of a stronger and more balanced inner world.

They act as a reminder of one's strengths and potential:

— **Building relationships:** In the aspect of building relationships, affirmations can be helpful in shaping a positive self-image and building healthy relationships with others. For instance, the affirmation "I am open and empathetic towards others" can support developing greater openness and the ability to form deeper connections. They also help overcome communication barriers, leading to a better understanding of oneself and others.

— **Dealing with challenges:** Affirmations are also a valuable tool in dealing with adversities and life challenges. Using affirmations like "I can find solutions even in difficult situations" allows maintaining a positive outlook, which translates into a greater ability to cope with problems and stressful situations.

— **Mental and emotional health:** In the area of mental and emotional health, affirmations are a supportive tool in building a stronger sense of self-worth and better well-being. Regular use of affirmations, such as "I appreciate myself and my achievements," often contributes to a higher level of life satisfaction and better emotional life quality. However, it's important to emphasize that affirmations complement, not replace, professional psychological help, especially in cases of more severe emotional issues.

History and Evolution of Affirmations

The history of affirmations dates back to antiquity, where they were an integral part of spiritual, religious, and therapeutic practices. In ancient Egypt, affirmations written in hieroglyphs were used in magical rituals, reflecting the belief in the power of words to influence reality. In the Vedic tradition of ancient India, mantras were considered vibrations resonating with the fundamental frequencies of the universe, playing a key role in spiritual practices.

Vedism is one of the oldest known religious-spiritual traditions, originating from the Indian subcontinent. The Vedas, the sacred scriptures of Vedism, are among the world's oldest religious texts. They were composed between 1500 and 500 BCE and played a central role in the development of Hinduism.

Vedic mantras were (and still are) considered sacred sounds or vibrations resonating with cosmic energies. They are used in various rituals and meditative practices, aiming to harmonize humans with the natural order of the universe.

In indigenous cultures, shamans used affirmations in the form of songs and spells for healing and spiritual purposes, which was part of everyday life and served a social and therapeutic role. In the philosophy of Stoicism and Epicureanism in ancient Greece and Rome, affirmations were recognized as a tool for shaping positive thinking and achieving a good life.

In the Middle Ages, within the context of Christianity, affirmations were used as part of prayer and meditation, serving as a tool for deepening faith and spiritual development. These early affirmations, rooted in religious beliefs and values, often took the form of prayerful repetitions or contemplations of the Holy Scriptures.

During the Enlightenment, with the arrival of a secular view of the world, affirmations began to evolve towards a personal development tool. Philosophers and thinkers such as Immanuel Kant and Jean-Jacques Rousseau emphasized the role of individual freedom and self-determination, significantly influencing the perception of affirmations. Their ideas contributed to a growing interest in using affirmations as a tool for personal development, highlighting their role in shaping positive self-esteem and independent thinking.

In the 20th century, with the development of positive psychology, affirmations gained popularity as a self-help tool. Psychologists like Abraham Maslow and Carl Rogers, focusing on the positive aspects of human nature, helped establish the role of affirmations in improving well-being and pursuing personal goals.

Today, affirmations are widely used in various contexts, from therapy to personal development training. They are utilized to work on one's beliefs, build a positive attitude, and achieve personal and professional goals. In positive psychology, affirmations are considered a tool supporting growth and development, focusing on leveraging internal potential and positive personality traits.

From ancient spiritual practices to modern psychology, affirmations have come a long way, evolving and adapting to the needs and beliefs of successive generations. Today's affirmations, although they may have roots in ancient practices, have been transformed and adapted to contemporary psychological frameworks, serving as a support tool in the pursuit of a fuller and more conscious life.

Chapter 2 — The Scientific Basis of Affirmations

Positive Psychology and Affirmations

Positive psychology, a psychological approach focused on potential, well-being, and the positive aspects of human experience, forms the foundation for the scientific understanding of affirmations. In this chapter, we will explore how research in positive psychology explains the mechanism of affirmations and why they can be an effective tool for personal development.

Understanding the Mechanism of Affirmations

Research in positive psychology has shown that affirmations can affect our brain and the way we think. Regular repetition of positive statements can lead to changes in brain areas responsible for self-regulation and positive thinking. Therefore, using affirmations can not only help in building positive self-esteem but also contribute to better coping with stress and life challenges.

According to self-affirmation theory (Steele, 1988), MRI evidence suggests that certain neural pathways are strengthened when individuals engage in self-affirmation tasks, such as daily repetition of positive affirmations. Additionally, it was found that self-affirmations can reduce health-damaging stress and are positively associated with academic achievements (Sherman et al., 2009; Layous et al., 2017).

Steele published the article "The Psychology of Self-Affirmation: Sustaining the Integrity of the Self" in "Advances in Experimental Social Psychology" in 1988, which laid the foundation for this theory.

A study conducted by Carnegie Mellon University investigated whether brief self-affirmations could alleviate the negative effects of chronic stress on problem-solving. The study used a measure of problem-solving and creativity (Remote Associates Task — RAT) to test three hypotheses: whether chronic stress is associated with poorer problem-solving, whether self-affirmation improves problem-solving, and whether these two main effects are moderated by the interaction of chronic stress and self-affirmation. Results confirmed that self-affirmation improves problem-solving among participants with high levels of chronic stress, (source:http://journals.plos.org/plosone/article?id=10.1371/journal.pone.0062593).

A study published in "Psychological Science" showed that affirmations change the way the brain's reward system operates, activating areas responsible for creating associations between positive stimuli and positive outcomes. Consequently, individuals with a positive self-image and strong sense of self-integrity can more strongly associate positive affirmations with desired outcomes.

The study titled: "Self-Affirmation Activates the Ventral Striatum: A Possible Reward-Related Mechanism for Self-Affirmation" was authored by Janine M. Dutcher, J. David Creswell, Laura E. Pacilio,

Peter R. Harris, William M. P. Klein, John M. Levine, Julienne E. Bower, Keely A. Muscatell, and Naomi I. Eisenberger. The study was published in April 2016 in the journal "Psychological Science".

Another study: "Self-affirmation activates brain systems associated with self-processing and reward, and is reinforced by a future orientation." was published in the journal "Social Cognitive and Affective Neuroscience" in April 2016. The study investigated the neural mechanisms of self-affirmation using functional magnetic resonance imaging (fMRI). It found that participants who underwent self-affirmation showed increased activity in brain areas associated with self-processing and valuation, especially when reflecting on core values oriented towards the future compared to everyday activities. This neural activity could predict changes in sedentary lifestyle, indicating effective self-affirmation in response to a physical activity intervention. The study provides insight into how self-affirmation can influence brain activity and behavior.

Affirmations in Therapeutic Practice

Beyond theoretical understanding, it is also important to look at the practical application of affirmations in therapy. Psychologists and therapists are increasingly incorporating affirmation techniques into their practice, helping clients build positive internal dialogue and cope with emotional challenges. It has been observed that they assist in achieving self-control through reflection on personal values and promote changes in health behaviors, such as healthier eating. They increase a sense of prosociality, reducing biases, for example, against members of minority groups.

How Does the Brain React to Affirmations?

Affirmations, or positive statements directed at oneself, aim to change thinking and attitudes. However, their effectiveness is not limited to conscious motivation. In fact, affirmations have a significant impact on the brain, as confirmed by neurological research.

Neuroplasticity and Affirmations

A key concept in understanding how the brain reacts to affirmations is neuroplasticity, or the brain's ability to change and adapt. When we regularly use affirmations, we can influence those areas of the brain responsible for self-awareness and self-regulation. By repeating positive statements, the brain begins to form new neural connections that reflect these positive thoughts.

The Effect of Affirmations on Brain Structures

Research using brain imaging, such as functional magnetic resonance imaging (fMRI), has shown that affirmations activate the same brain regions as other positive emotional stimuli. Activated areas include the anterior cingulate cortex, a region associated with positive emotions and self-esteem. Regular use of affirmations can strengthen these areas, which in turn contributes to an increase in positive emotions and enhanced self-confidence.

Affirmations and the Brain's Reward System

Another interesting aspect is the interaction of affirmations with the brain's reward system. Repeating positive statements can activate brain areas responsible for experiencing pleasure, such as the nucleus accumbens. This may explain why affirmations often evoke feelings of satisfaction and well-being.

Long-term Effects of Affirmations

Long-term use of affirmations can contribute to lasting changes in the brain. Through regular reinforcement of positive beliefs, we can gradually change dominant thought patterns, which translates into long-term improvement in well-being and a positive attitude towards life.

Understanding how the brain reacts to affirmations shows that these tools have a real and measurable impact on our neurological functions. From neuroplasticity to the activation of the reward system, affirmations can be a powerful tool in the pursuit of positive change and personal development.

Chapter 3 — Mistakes in Using Affirmations

Why Don't Affirmations Always Work?

Many people, raised in an educational system that rarely emphasizes personal development and self-awareness, do not understand the complexity of affirmations. Affirmations are not just about repeating positive statements; they are a tool that requires a deep understanding of one's own emotions, beliefs, and subconscious.

The lack of education about affirmations in schools means that many individuals are unaware of how important it is to understand their own inner world before starting affirmation practice. Education should include not only learning about affirmations but also about how our thoughts and beliefs shape our reality, and the role of the subconscious in the process of change.

Effective use of affirmations requires a high level of self-awareness and self-knowledge. An individual must be aware of their internal blocks, beliefs, and emotional reactions. Without this knowledge, affirmations may be ineffective because they do not address deeper underlying issues and beliefs.

There are common misconceptions that affirmations are a magical formula that can instantly change life. This approach overlooks the need for deep self-work and understanding of the processes occurring in the mind. Affirmations are a tool that, when used correctly, can support the personal development process but do not replace it.

A key aspect of effective affirmations is working with the subconscious. Most of our beliefs and behavior patterns are rooted in the subconscious, so merely repeating affirmations on a conscious level often isn't enough to bring about lasting change. Deeper work is needed to reach and change these ingrained beliefs.

Affirmations should be part of a broader personal development process that also includes techniques such as meditation, introspection, and working with a therapist or coach. Only when they are part of a holistic approach to growth and development can they yield the expected results.

In summary, the lack of education and understanding of the mechanism of affirmations leads to their improper use and disappointments. For affirmations to be effective, a deep understanding of subconscious processes, self-awareness, and integration with an overall personal development process is necessary.

Internal Conflicts and Lack of Emotional Alignment

In the practice of affirmations, the authenticity of emotions plays a key role. Often, people face failures in using affirmations not because the affirmations themselves are ineffective, but due to internal conflicts. When someone tries to convince themselves of their worth while deep down feeling unworthy, it creates an emotional conflict. This lack of emotional alignment is a common reason for failure.

In such cases, an affirmation may act like a mask covering the true feelings. For instance, a person repeating "I am strong and independent," while feeling deep fear and uncertainty, will struggle to achieve positive results. This is because affirmations are not a magic wand but a tool that requires consistency between the conscious mind and deeply rooted emotions and beliefs.

Forcing oneself to think positively when internally feeling something entirely different is not only ineffective but can be harmful. Ignoring one's doubts, fears, and genuine emotions leads to their suppression, which over time can cause greater emotional problems. Affirmations should be used as part of a broader process of acceptance and self-understanding, not as an attempt to erase or ignore negative feelings.

The key to effectively using affirmations is, therefore, to start by working on internal conflicts and contradictions. This means confronting one's fears, doubts, and negative beliefs. Affirmations can be a powerful tool in the process of change, but only when paired with deep personal work.

Thus, instead of using affirmations as a way to "cover up" negative feelings, they should be utilized as part of the process of getting to know and accepting oneself. Affirmations can become a bridge connecting what we feel inside with what we wish to achieve, when they are in line with our true emotional and spiritual path.

Life Examples from My Students:

Example 1: Career and Self-Esteem

Ania, an ambitious professional, one day began the process of affirmations and started repeating to herself: "I am competent and successful at my work." Despite this, deep down she struggled with imposter syndrome, believing that her achievements were the result of luck, not skill. This emotional inconsistency meant that the affirmation, instead of boosting her confidence, effectively deepened her internal belief of insufficiency. Ania felt increasingly fraudulent and uneasy, despite external signs of success.

Example 2: Relationships and Self-Worth

Tomasz, after a series of failed relationships, tried to convince himself: "I am valuable and deserve love." However, internally, he still felt rejected and unworthy. Each new relationship quickly ended because his deeply rooted beliefs sabotaged the ability to build healthy, stable connections. Despite affirming positive beliefs about himself, his internal beliefs created a wall that was hard to break through.

Example 3: Finances and Sense of Security

Ewa, trying to improve her financial situation, repeated daily: "I am financially independent, and abundance flows to me easily." Nevertheless, she continued to experience deep-seated fear related to money, stemming from a difficult childhood where she constantly faced scarcity. This fear caused her, despite her efforts, to be unable to effectively manage her finances and to approach investment opportunities with mistrust, preventing her from achieving true financial independence.

In these examples, the key element is the inconsistency between the affirmed words and deeply rooted beliefs and emotions. <u>For affirmations to be effective, it is necessary to work on resolving these internal conflicts first.</u>

The Subconscious Reaction to Misapplication of Affirmations

The subconscious plays a pivotal role in the affirmation process, yet it often initially resists. This resistance is primarily due to the subconscious tendency to maintain the status quo, protecting us from what it perceives as unknown or potentially dangerous. Moreover, long-standing beliefs and thought patterns rooted in our subconscious may conflict with new affirmations. When we attempt to introduce change through affirmations, our subconscious might react negatively, perceiving it as a threat to the known order.

Delving into the psychological and neurological aspects of subconscious operation, the resistance mechanism of the subconscious against change is rooted in the brain's evolutionary defense mechanism. The brain, especially its more primitive parts like the limbic system, is programmed to avoid danger and maintain homeostasis—a state of equilibrium and stability. Changes, even positive ones, can be perceived as a threat to this balance.

— Daniel Kahneman, a Nobel Prize laureate in economics, discusses in his book two systems of thinking—fast and slow. System 1 (fast) is automatic and operates on a subconscious level, while System 2 (slow) is deliberate, conscious, and requires effort. The subconscious (System 1) often resists changes proposed by the conscious part of the mind (System 2) due to its automaticity and resistance to the effort of change.

Thinking, Fast and Slow by Daniel Kahneman was published by Farrar, Straus and Giroux in 2011.

— The works of Joseph LeDoux, a specialist in emotional neuroscience, show how our brain reacts to fear and threat. His research confirms how deeply ingrained defensive reactions in the limbic system affect our ability to process and adapt to new experiences, including affirmations. LeDoux is the author of many books and scientific articles on the neurobiology of emotions. Among his most well-known publications are *The Emotional Brain: The Mysterious Underpinnings of Emotional Life* and *Synaptic Self: How Our Brains Become Who We Are*.

— *The Power of Habit* by Charles Duhigg: In his book, Duhigg discusses how habits are formed and solidified in our brain. He describes the process of creating a habit loop, emphasizing how difficult it is to change entrenched behavior patterns, which is directly related to the subconscious resistance to change. *The Power of Habit: Why We Do What We Do in Life and Business* by Charles Duhigg was published by Random House Trade Paperbacks in February 2012.

— *Subliminal: How Your Unconscious Mind Rules Your Behavior* by Leonard Mlodinow: Mlodinow explores how our subconscious shapes our decisions, thoughts, and feelings. He highlights that many of our subconscious processes are resistant to conscious change. *Subliminal: How Your Unconscious Mind Rules Your Behavior* by Leonard Mlodinow was published by Random House in 2012.

— Research on brain plasticity: New studies in the field of neuroplasticity show that our brain is capable of change and adaptation throughout our lives. However, these changes require conscious effort and time, which contradicts the brain's natural tendency to maintain the status quo.

In summary, the subconscious resistance to change is deeply ingrained in our biological and psychological functioning. Understanding this process is crucial in working with affirmations and striving for personal development, and recognizing the role of the subconscious in affirmations is extremely important. For affirmations to be effective, they must align with our deep beliefs and emotions. There can be no contradiction. The symbiosis between consciously creating affirmations and subconscious beliefs is key to achieving positive change.

How the Subconscious Processes Affirmations

The subconscious processes affirmations in a manner somewhat similar to how we learn a foreign language or how to ride a bicycle. Initially, it is difficult because our mind is not yet familiar with the new pattern of thinking we are trying to introduce through affirmations.

As we repeat affirmations, the subconscious gradually begins to assimilate them, but this process does not happen instantly. Initially, the subconscious may resist because it prefers to stick to what it already knows and considers safe, even if those are negative beliefs. Over time, if we consistently repeat affirmations, the subconscious begins to accept them as a new reality.

It's a bit like convincing a good friend of a new idea. At first, they may be skeptical, but if you regularly talk about it and show that it works, eventually they will start to believe it. It is also important that affirmations align with our feelings. If we express something we completely do not feel, our subconscious will quickly detect this and treat it as a false alarm.

Therefore, it's crucial that affirmations are realistic and gradually lead us to change, rather than trying to change everything overnight by 180 degrees. It's a bit like planting a flower — we need time, regular care, and patience to see it grow and bloom.

Emotions

Emotions reside in the subconscious because they are part of a deeply ingrained information processing system in the brain that operates below the level of our conscious awareness.

Our subconscious acts as a storage for automatic reactions, beliefs, and experiences that have been shaped throughout our life. Emotional responses often are automatic and occur without conscious thought, for example, the feeling of fear in response to a threat is immediate and does not require conscious deliberation.

The subconscious helps to protect our psyche by storing emotions that might be too painful or difficult to process consciously. Defense mechanisms, such as repression, allow hiding these emotions in deeper layers of the mind. The subconscious continuously processes our experiences, including the associated emotions, even when we are not aware of it, which helps us learn and develop based on our experiences.

Emotions in the subconscious often serve as an instinctive guide, helping us make decisions and respond to the environment in a way that is not always conscious but is based on previous experiences and inner intuition. They are also a form of communication between the subconscious and the conscious part of the mind, often signaling our deeply rooted needs, desires, and fears.

Understanding the role of the subconscious in storing and processing emotions is crucial in many aspects of personal development, including working with affirmations, giving us a better understanding of ourselves and a more effective influence on our reality.

When emotions are aligned with the affirmed message, they act as reinforcement, adding credibility and power to the statements. For example, if you say "I am full of energy and enthusiasm," and you truly feel that way, then this affirmation is significantly stronger. Your body and mind are in harmony, working together to make this statement a reality.

Conversely, if your emotions conflict with the affirmation, they can weaken or even negate its effect. Imagine a situation where you repeat: "I am happy," but in reality, you feel sadness. This discrepancy between words and emotions creates an internal conflict that is subconsciously perceived as untrue or forced.

In such a case, it is first necessary to identify the source, the reason for your sadness, and direct your analysis there. It may turn out that understanding, forgiveness, or healing is needed — this is a matter of individual necessity. It might be necessary to seek the help of a therapist or psychologist. Later, steps can be taken to overwrite the positive affirmation.

Emotions in such situations are very helpful because they can reveal hidden blocks and limitations. For example, if you notice that certain affirmations trigger discomfort, fear, or resistance, this could be a signal that deeper, unprocessed fears, traumas, habits, or beliefs lie behind them.

In summary, emotions significantly affect the effectiveness of affirmations. For their efficacy, it is crucial that the accompanying feelings are authentic and in harmony with the content of the affirmation. Understanding and harmonizing one's own emotions, therefore, constitute an essential aspect of the affirmation process.

Life Examples from My Students:

Example 1: Changing Jobs

Marta, who had worked in a stable but undemanding job for years, began to affirm: "I am capable of finding a job that inspires and develops me." Her subconscious, accustomed to safety and routine, began to evoke fear of the unknown, restraining her from actively searching for new opportunities. Instead of feeling motivated, Marta felt increasingly overwhelmed.

Example 2: Improving Self-Esteem

Jakub, struggling with low self-esteem, started using the affirmation: "I am valuable and deserve respect." His subconscious, filled with negative beliefs from childhood, raised doubts in him, making every attempt to strengthen his self-esteem end with a feeling of falseness and disbelief in those words.

Example 3: Healthy Lifestyle

Ewelina, aiming for a healthier lifestyle, began to affirm: "I choose healthy food and regular exercise." However, her subconscious, deeply rooted in the habits and comforts of her previous lifestyle, caused strong resistance. Ewelina often found excuses not to exercise or reached for unhealthy snacks, despite her conscious effort to change.

In each of these cases, before affirmations can bring the expected results, it is necessary to work on resolving conflicts and resistances coming from the subconscious.

Incorrect Autosuggestion Weakens the Effectiveness of Affirmations

What is Autosuggestion?

The term "autosuggestion" was popularized by Émile Coué, a French psychologist and pharmacist, in the early 20th century. Coué, who lived from 1857 to 1926, was a pioneer in the application of autosuggestion in self-help and personal development. His approach, known as the Coué method, was based on the belief that repeating certain positive phrases could lead to self-fulfilling prophecies and changes in a person's beliefs or behaviors. The most famous example of Coué's autosuggestion is the affirmation: *"Day by day, in every way, I'm getting better and better."* The Coué method had an impact on the development of many later techniques in the field of positive psychology and self-improvement.

Autosuggestion is the process by which we convince ourselves of certain things. It's as if you continually told yourself that you are good at something or that something will succeed. It can be compared to an internal monologue that shapes our beliefs and influences how we perceive ourselves and the world around us.

An example of autosuggestion might be the scene where, before an important event, you convince yourself that you will manage and everything will go well. Your thoughts and what you repeat to yourself have the power to influence your emotions and behaviors. It's a bit like programming your own mind for positive thinking or achieving goals.

Improper form of autosuggestion can significantly reduce the effectiveness of affirmations. When we talk about autosuggestion, it refers to the process in which we convince ourselves of certain thoughts or beliefs. If this is done incorrectly, instead of helping, it can have the opposite effect.

Suppose someone repeats an affirmation that sounds unnatural or is contrary to their deep beliefs. This can evoke internal resistance and reinforce negative thoughts. For example, telling oneself "I am wealthy" when struggling with finances can trigger feelings of inconsistency and falsehood.

Additionally, if autosuggestion is too general or vague, it may not effectively influence the subconscious. Affirmations should be personalized, realistic, and precise to properly impact our thoughts and behaviors.

In short, improper form of autosuggestion can make affirmations ineffective or even worsen our thinking and well-being, instead of improving it.

Fictional Examples of Incorrect Forms of Autosuggestion:

— *Inconsistency with Reality: Tom is a student and has financial troubles. He begins to repeat to himself daily: "I am a millionaire." Instead of feeling better, Tomek becomes increasingly frustrated because his reality does not match what he is trying to convince himself of.*

— *Too General Statements: Anna wants to improve her well-being and starts using the affirmation: "I am happy." However, she does not specify what exactly makes her happy, so her mind does not know how to interpret and apply this affirmation in specific situations.*

— *Lack of Belief in What Is Said: Kate wants to be more confident and tells herself every day: "I am confident." Deep down, however, she still feels insecure, and her subconscious treats these words as untrue, rendering the affirmation ineffective.*

— *Negative Associations: Paul, who wants to quit smoking, repeats to himself: "I don't need cigarettes." However, each use of the word "cigarettes" makes him think about them even more, increasing his desire to smoke.*

— Too Ambitious Goals: Eve aims to lose 15 kg and repeats to herself daily: "I lose 15 kg in a month." This goal is unrealistic and overly ambitious, causing Ewa to quickly lose motivation when she does not see rapid results.

In each of these cases, the improper use of autosuggestion causes the affirmations not only to fail in bringing the desired effects but can even induce additional stress and frustration.

Negations

Negations such as "not" can be less effective in affirmations because authenticity and positive phrasing are key to their efficacy.

An affirmation like "I am not in debt" may be less effective for several reasons related to the functioning of the subconscious and the way language is processed. The subconscious focuses on key words in a sentence, often overlooking negations. In the case of the affirmation "I am not in debt," the key word is "debt," which may lead to an unwanted focus on debt, rather than its absence.

The subconscious operates on the principle of images and associations. Words and sentences are interpreted by it literally, without analysis of their contextual or logical meaning. For this reason, affirmations should be formulated in a direct, positive, and negation-free manner, so the subconscious can properly process and reinforce them.

For example, instead of the affirmation "I am not in debt," a more effective phrase might be "I am financially free" or "My reality is financial stability."

This way, we focus the subconscious's attention on the positive aspect—financial freedom or stability, not on debt.

In practice, this means that when formulating affirmations, one should avoid negative words and focus on statements that are positive, clear, and direct. This allows for a better rooting of desired beliefs and goals in the subconscious, which can contribute to more effective changes in thinking and action.

Chapter 4 — Negative Beliefs and Blockages

In this chapter, we'll discuss the mental barriers and blockages I've most commonly encountered in my work as a therapist.

Here are a few of them:

— **Belief in the Ineffectiveness of Affirmations**: Many people assume that affirmations are just empty words without any real impact on reality. This belief may stem from previous unsuccessful attempts at using affirmations or from a lack of understanding of how they work.

— **Lack of Self-Belief**: A common blockage is the belief that we don't deserve success, happiness, or change. Internal dialogues like *"I am not good enough"* or *"I don't deserve this"* pose a significant obstacle to the effective use of affirmations.

— **Fear of Change**: Often, a subconscious fear of change and leaving the comfort zone paralyzes the affirmation process. People are afraid of what will happen if their lives actually begin to change.

— **Skepticism and Cynicism**: A skeptical and cynical attitude towards affirmations as a method of personal development can result from cultural or social beliefs, as well as negative past experiences.

— **Negative Thought Habits**: Long-standing negative thought patterns, such as pessimism, excessive self-criticism, or generalizing negative experiences, can block the effectiveness of affirmations.

— **Lack of Patience and Consistency**: Many people expect quick results and give up on affirmations when they don't see immediate changes. A lack of patience and consistency in practice is a major obstacle.

— **Unconscious Beliefs**: Deeply rooted, unconscious beliefs, often acquired in childhood, may be in conflict with the content of affirmations, leading to their ineffectiveness.

Recognizing and understanding these negative beliefs and blockages is the first step to overcoming them and effectively using affirmations.

Negative beliefs act like a saboteur in the affirmation process. Imagine your affirmations as a boat sailing down a river, and negative beliefs as holes in this boat. No matter how hard you try to move forward, these holes constantly allow water inside and slow your progress, or even cause you to start sinking.

For example, you tell yourself *"I am a successful entrepreneur,"* but deep down, you hold the belief *"I will never make it."* It's like trying to drive a car with one foot on the gas and the other on the brake. These internal conflicts mean you remain stationary.

How Can You Identify and Eliminate Blockages?

The first step is self-awareness.

Start by paying attention to your thoughts. When negative ones emerge, write them down. It's a bit like a detective gathering evidence.

Next, try to understand where they came from. Often, negative beliefs are rooted in the past, for example, in childhood or previous experiences. Ask yourself: "Why do I think this way? Is it true, or just an old script I'm replaying?"

After identifying these beliefs, you can start working on them. One method is to confront them and replace them with more positive and realistic thoughts. You can also try techniques such as meditation, visualization, or working with a therapist to address deeper issues.

Remember, changing negative beliefs is a process. It doesn't happen overnight, but with time and practice, significant improvement can be achieved.

Affirmations and Self-Esteem

The distorted self-esteem of many people today results from a series of factors that make up our complex social and cultural environment. The modern world is characterized by immense pressure on achievements, appearance, and social status, which often translates into self-worth.

Social media plays a significant role, often presenting unrealistic images of life and success. People are bombarded with images of perfect lives, attractiveness, and achievements, which can lead to comparisons with others and feelings of inadequacy. Constant comparison with others, especially on social media, can lead to low self-esteem and the feeling that one does not meet expectations.

Additionally, the contemporary culture of success and efficiency at work and in personal life puts people under constant pressure. Expectations of continual achievement, being the best, and constant personal development can be overwhelming and negatively affect self-esteem, especially when people feel they do not meet these standards.

Education and upbringing also play a role. The way children are raised and educated can significantly affect their later self-esteem. Excessive criticism, lack of emotional support, or too high expectations can lead to feelings of not being good enough.

Moreover, the changing and uncertain world we live in, with its economic, social, and environmental challenges, also affects people's well-being and self-esteem. Uncertainty about the future, concerns about financial security, and health can influence how people see themselves and their place in the world.

As a result, the combination of these factors can lead to disturbed self-esteem in many people, especially in the context of constant bombardment with messages and images that are often unrealistic and unattainable.

Affirmations improve self-esteem and self-worth by changing negative internal dialogue to positive. Regularly repeating positive statements about oneself helps transform internal beliefs and approach to life. What initially may seem like just words, over time, begins to affect the way of thinking, changing negative thought patterns into more positive and constructive ones.

This process is supported by the brain's ability to adapt and change. Moreover, affirmations often increase self-awareness and focus on personal values and goals.

They reduce stress and anxiety levels, which directly affects self-worth. When people feel less stressed and worried, they tend to view themselves in a better light. Reducing negative emotions allows for a more objective and positive view of oneself and one's achievements.

As a result, regular use of affirmations can lead to profound and lasting changes in how people perceive themselves and their value, translating into improved self-esteem and overall well-being.

Affirmations as Choosing a New Path, Not Striving for Perfection

In today's times, where the culture of perfection and excellence is ubiquitous, it's easy to fall into the belief that we need to "fix" something within ourselves through affirmations or other personal development techniques. However, this approach diverts attention from the true value of affirmations.

The first step should be understanding that each of us is already perfect in our unique essence. Every moment of our lives is the best version of ourselves. The awareness that we are already complete, and our imperfections are part of our unique identity, is the foundation of genuine development.

In this context, affirmations are not a tool for "fixing" oneself but are a way to choose a new life path. They serve to change direction, not to pursue some idealized image of perfection. By using affirmations, we focus on developing our potentials and exploring new aspects of our selves, rather than on constant self-improvement.

It's important to understand that seeking perfection is a road to nowhere. Perfectionism often leads to frustration and a sense of inadequacy because there will always be something that could be done better. Meanwhile, affirmations should serve self-acceptance and embracing our lives as they are, as well as opening up to new possibilities and experiences.

By adopting affirmations as a tool for choosing new paths, rather than a means to strive for unrealistic ideals, we open ourselves to true growth. This allows us to live more fully, with greater self-awareness and an understanding of our true desires.

In this light, affirmations become not just a method of personal development but also a path to deeper self-understanding and awareness of the world around us. They are an invitation to a life that is more authentic, fulfilled, and free from the burden of striving for unattainable standards of perfection.

As you can see, I have dedicated many pages of this book to show you the most common mistakes and traps that can occur with the improper use of affirmations.

Perhaps you've noticed that some of them have also occurred in your practice. I hope that now, armed with this knowledge, you will look at affirmations from a new perspective.

In the following chapters, we will focus on the positive aspects of affirmations, so you can fully utilize this powerful tool for self-development and introducing positive changes into your life. I invite you to continue reading, full of inspiration and practical tips.

Chapter 5 — Practices for Building Self-Confidence

Building self-confidence can be achieved through a variety of practices and exercises that focus on personal development and self-awareness, not just affirmations.

Here are a few examples:

— Begin your day with a few minutes of meditation or mindfulness, focusing on your thoughts and emotions. This enhances self-awareness and inner peace, helping you better understand yourself and your needs.

— Keep a journal in which you record your achievements, successes, and positive experiences. Focusing on the positive aspects of life strengthens your sense of self-worth.

— Engage in regular physical activity. Not only does this improve physical health, but also mental health, and team sports or fitness classes can help in building social relationships.

— Practice setting small, achievable goals for yourself. Accomplishing these goals step by step increases your sense of competence and control over your life.

— Practice the skill of assertiveness, learning to express your thoughts and needs in a clear and respectful manner. This improves social interactions and strengthens your sense of self-worth.

— Take up a hobby or activity that brings you joy and allows you to develop skills and passions. This provides a sense of achievement and allows for a break from daily stresses.

— Practice gratitude, for example by writing down things you are grateful for each day. This changes your approach to life and helps focus on the positive aspects of your experience.

— Consider joining groups focused on personal development, such as yoga, tai chi, or Pilates. Joining such a group offers many benefits. Regular participation in classes allows for better control over your body and mind, which translates into greater self-awareness.

These practices combine physical, mental, and spiritual aspects. Participating in groups allows meeting people with similar interests, which affects well-being and self-perception. Moreover, regular exercises bring health benefits, such as stress reduction and improved flexibility.

The activities listed, when practiced regularly, can gradually build self-confidence, aiding in the development of a positive self-image and effective coping with everyday life challenges.

How to Create Effective Affirmations?

Understanding Your Limitations and Challenges.

Understanding your own limitations and challenges is crucial when working with affirmations. Trying to instill positive beliefs through the "closed doors" of internal blockages, our words lose their potential. Often, these blockages are unconscious negative beliefs rooted in our experiences. For instance, if we were told in childhood that we are not good at something, that voice might stay with us, shaping our beliefs about ourselves. Similarly, repeated failures in a field can lead to a belief in a lack of talent, even if the reasons lie elsewhere — in the wrong approach or a lack of learning tools. Understanding and addressing these internal limitations is the first step to creating effective affirmations.

The most challenging are negative beliefs rooted in childhood or the distant past, often evolving into internal limitations that effectively hinder our development. It is therefore crucial to consciously recognize and work on them. Without this effort, even the most effective affirmations may encounter internal resistance, saying, "this is not for me, I can't do this."

Various forms of internal limitations, like fear of change or belief in a lack of merit for success, require an individual approach. Understanding their origin, often with the help of a therapist or coach, is the first step to overcoming them.

Once you identify your barriers, such as an internal belief in a lack of merit for success, you can apply specific affirmations. For example, affirmations like "I am worthy of success and happiness in life" can help strengthen self-esteem and a sense of deserving.

Remember, affirmations are not just words but also the emotions they evoke. If your affirmations are not in agreement with your feelings, their effectiveness can be limited. Therefore, it's important to work on your emotional limitations concurrently, allowing affirmations to fully function.

Self-improvement takes time and patience but yields significant results. Noticing how your thinking changes and how you start achieving goals, you will see the value of this work. Affirmations are a powerful tool, most effective when used by someone aware of their internal limitations and actively working on them.

However, it's worth noting that in some situations, affirmations alone may prove insufficient. In such cases, seeking professional help from a therapist or psychologist, who can assist in deeper understanding and working through those internal barriers hindering our development and well-being, is key.

Acceptance and Letting Go Techniques: Learning to accept the current situation as a starting point for change.

Acceptance and letting go techniques teach how to cope with the current situation, instead of fighting it or pretending the problems don't exist. It's about accepting reality as it is now. Letting go means giving up holding onto old thoughts and emotions that pull us down.

This enables us to experience peace, as accepting the current situation paradoxically makes it easier for us to make changes. This process begins with mindfulness, being more aware of our thoughts and feelings, and not automatically reacting to everything that comes up.

And now, how this ties into affirmations: for them to be effective, we first need to accept where we currently are. Acceptance and letting go techniques are like preparing the soil for affirmations. First, we learn to accept and let go, then we introduce affirmations, which work better because we're more open to change.

They can be applied simultaneously, learning to accept and using affirmations to support this process. There's no rule that says they shouldn't be used together. In fact, they can complement each other very well, creating a comprehensive approach that aids in development and goal achievement.

<u>Techniques for Reducing Negative Emotions: Methods to minimize negative feelings that can weaken the power of affirmations.</u>

Techniques for alleviating negative emotions are invaluable for those grappling with emotional barriers or raised in an atmosphere of pessimism.

Among these methods, affirmations, though effective, often encounter a wall of resistance. This resistance stems from deeply rooted, negative beliefs that stand in stark contrast to the positive message of affirmations.

The often-present discrepancy between the actual state and the aspirations affirmations try to instill can be a source of frustration. Individuals accustomed to a negative view of reality may experience inner discomfort, and even a sense of being misled, when faced with the challenge of accepting positive statements. This natural reaction results from perceiving affirmations as contradictory to long-established, pessimistic beliefs.

In practice, confronting affirmations can be likened to attempting to navigate uncharted waters. On one hand, there is a desire to change course towards positive thinking, and on the other, a strong attachment to the safe, yet limiting, harbor of negative beliefs. This process requires time, patience, and often, a transformation of internal dialogue.

To tackle this challenge, several methods can be useful:

— Understanding and accepting your own emotions: The first step is to realize that negative feelings are a natural part of the change process. It's important not to judge yourself for experiencing them but rather to accept them as an element of your own development.

— Gradually introducing affirmations: Instead of trying to adopt very positive statements right away, start with those that are neutral and gradually modify them. For example, instead of saying "I am happy," begin with "I am striving to be happier each day."

— Relaxation techniques: Meditation, deep breathing, or yoga can help calm the mind and better cope with negative emotions. When the mind is calmer, it's easier to accept positive thoughts.

— Emotion journal: Keeping a journal where you write down your feelings and thoughts can help understand why negative reactions to affirmations arise. This tool allows for better self-knowledge and understanding of your thought patterns.

— Working with a therapist: For those struggling to overcome emotional blocks, professional help can be very valuable. A therapist can help understand the reasons behind negative thinking and suggest individually tailored coping techniques.

— Mindfulness exercises: Practicing mindfulness, being present at the moment, and aware of your experiences, can help reduce stress levels and better deal with negative thoughts.

Understanding that changing entrenched thought patterns takes time and patience is key. Negative feelings won't disappear overnight, but regularly applying the mentioned techniques can greatly assist in minimizing them and increasing the effectiveness of affirmations.

Clarity and Specificity

A key aspect is articulating your vision in a clear and specific manner. Thanks to clarity and specificity, the mind more easily absorbs and implements positive affirmations.

An affirmation should be direct, understandable, and precise. Avoid generalities that can introduce ambiguities and be difficult to interpret.

A clear and specific affirmation is more convincing and effective. The mind responds better to messages that are direct and understandable. For example, instead of saying "I will be happier," it is better to say "I feel joy every day through my hobbies." Such an affirmation is not only precise but also relates to the present, which makes it easier for the mind to accept.

The clarity of an affirmation helps focus on a specific goal. This makes it easier to direct thoughts and energy in the desired direction. Specificity makes the goal seem realistic and achievable, which increases motivation and commitment. Focusing on specific aspects of life that we want to improve facilitates the identification and execution of necessary steps.

A clear affirmation facilitates the visualization of the desired outcome. When we have a clear image of the goal in our mind, it is easier to imagine changes in our life. Clear affirmations are like guides in daily life, helping maintain course towards goals, even during difficulties. They provide a sense of purpose and direction, which is key for lasting changes.

Using clear affirmations also affects the subconscious. Regularly repeating specific, positive statements influences subconscious beliefs and attitudes. This leads to changes in behavior and thinking, which is essential for long-term success and goal achievement.

A well-formulated affirmation should be thoughtful, clear, and focused on a specific aspect of life that we wish to improve or change.

Examples:

1. Incorrect Affirmation: "I will be happier in the future."

Why It's Ineffective: This affirmation is too general and not time-specific. It doesn't specify when or under what circumstances the person will be happier, making it difficult for the mind to assimilate.

Correct Version: "I am happy every day, enjoying the little things."

The correct form of affirmation, "I am happy every day, enjoying the little things," is effective because it focuses on the current experience of happiness. Instead of deferring the feeling of happiness to an undefined future, it expresses a sense of contentment that is experienced regularly in daily life. Focusing on the little things as a source of happiness is a concrete and realistic approach that can be easily integrated into daily life. This affirmation aids in grounding a positive mindset and appreciating the present moments, conducive to building a lasting sense of happiness. This statement is also direct and personal, enhancing its resonance and effectiveness in shaping a positive state of mind.

2. Incorrect Affirmation: "My life will be better."

Why It's Ineffective: This is too generic a statement that does not specify what exactly "a better life" means. The lack of specificity makes it hard for the subconscious to accept such an affirmation as real.

Correct Version: "Every day, I take specific actions to improve my relationships and health."

The correct affirmation, "Every day, I take specific actions to improve my relationships and health," is effective because it specifies exact areas of life the person is working on—relationships and health. It focuses on daily actions, which are realistic and give a sense of control over one's life. Instead of a vague and distant goal of "a better life," it emphasizes current, active efforts that are measurable and conducted with awareness. Such an affirmation helps in grounding habits and behaviors that contribute to improving the quality of life. It is a practical, action-focused approach, increasing the likelihood of real change and a positive impact on the individual's life.

3. Incorrect Affirmation: "I will have more money."

Why It's Ineffective: This affirmation does not specify how and when the person will have more money, making it less believable and difficult to realize.

Correct Version: "I effectively manage my finances and save regularly."

The correct affirmation, "I effectively manage my finances and save regularly," is effective because it specifically outlines actions related to managing finances. Instead of an undefined and vague idea of having more money, this affirmation focuses on real and concrete actions, such as effective financial management and regular saving. This approach helps in forming practical habits directly related to improving one's financial situation.

Such a statement facilitates achieving financial goals because it engages the individual in active and conscious action, rather than leaving them in a state of waiting for an uncertain future change. This affirmation promotes a sense of responsibility and control over one's finances, which is crucial for achieving financial stability and well-being.

Present Tense

Creating affirmations in the present tense plays a crucial role in personal development and effectively achieving change. Such a form of affirmation allows for the immediate visualization and experience of the desired changes, avoiding the postponement of these changes into an uncertain future. Moreover, our subconscious more easily accepts thoughts expressed in the present tense, treating them as real events rather than just distant goals.

Our subconscious operates on the principles of immediacy and simplicity. Affirmations in the present tense are simpler and more direct, which facilitates their assimilation by the mind, provided there are no strong emotional blockades. Unlike affirmations focused on the future, which are often abstract, statements in the present tense are perceived as more real. As a result, they are more easily accepted as part of the current experience.

Regular repetition of affirmations in the present tense can influence the brain's neuroplasticity, that is, its ability to change and adapt. This aids in reconfiguring neural pathways and allows the brain to adopt new, positive patterns of thinking. Such affirmations can also increase motivation to act now, not postponing it for later. The belief that we already possess the desired traits or achievements can inspire us to take specific actions to realize them.

Affirmations are most effective when they are in line with our emotions. When the emotions expressed in affirmations are authentic and match our inner beliefs, then they are not a form of self-deception but a conscious shaping of a positive attitude. Affirmations do not have to be perceived as literal statements of truth but can serve as tools for shaping our way of thinking and feeling, helping to break negative patterns and build a more positive self-image. It is important that they are realistic and aligned with our values and beliefs, which enhances their effectiveness.

Examples:

1. Incorrect Affirmation: "I will be satisfied with my job when I get a promotion."

— *Why It's Ineffective:* This affirmation postpones the feeling of satisfaction to the future and makes it dependent on achieving a specific goal, which can lead to a perpetual sense of dissatisfaction and waiting.

— *Correct Version:* "I feel satisfaction and contentment with my current job and the contributions I make."

The correct form of affirmation, such as "I feel satisfaction and contentment with my current job and the contributions I make," brings numerous benefits. Declaring satisfaction with one's current job strengthens positive well-being, contributing to an increase in internal self-worth, which is essential for mental health.

Such an affirmation encourages increased motivation and engagement in tasks since the feeling of satisfaction with work encourages putting in greater effort and enthusiasm. As a result, it may lead to better professional outcomes.

This affirmation also supports creating a positive self-image as a competent and satisfied employee. It's important to remember that self-perception often influences our actions and effectiveness.

Focusing on the realistic perception of the current situation, it is realistic and achievable. Its use increases the likelihood of a positive impact on the individual's life. Practicing this affirmation can not only raise the sense of satisfaction and efficacy in the current job but also unconsciously contribute to creating conditions favorable for promotion and further professional development.

2. Incorrect Affirmation: "Someday I will find the love of my life."

— Why It's Ineffective: This affirmation pushes the possibility of finding love into an undefined future, which can perpetuate a sense of lack and loneliness.

— Correct Version: "I am open and ready for love in my life now."

The correct affirmation "I am open and ready for love in my life now" is effective for several reasons. First and foremost, it focuses on the current state of readiness and openness to love, which is key. Unlike postponing love to an uncertain future, this affirmation expresses readiness to accept love in the present.

This approach fosters a positive attitude towards romantic relationships, creating an internal space to experience love now, instead of waiting for it in an undefined future time.

This statement also significantly impacts changing personal attitudes, as affirming readiness for love not only declares an open heart but also emphasizes readiness to create healthy, loving relationships.

Such an attitude can attract positive circumstances, opening the individual to new possibilities in their emotional life. Additionally, this affirmation can help overcome any internal blockages or fears related to forming deep connections, which is often necessary for fully opening up to love.

As a result, the person using this affirmation may not only feel more open to love but also actively work on creating conditions conducive to building and maintaining healthy romantic relationships.

3. Incorrect Affirmation: "I will be healthy when I start exercising more and eating better."

— *Why It's Ineffective*: *It shifts responsibility for health to future actions, which can lead to postponing changes over time.*

— *Correct Version*: *"I care for my health every day through physical activity and healthy eating."*

The correct affirmation "I care for my health every day through physical activity and healthy eating" is effective because it emphasizes direct actions and commitments towards health. Instead of postponing health care to the future and making it dependent on uncertain future actions, this affirmation actively acknowledges and affirms ongoing efforts towards a healthy lifestyle.

Highlighting current care for health is crucial because it aids in creating and maintaining healthy habits. This approach supports building a positive attitude towards one's health and well-being, which is key for lasting change and the development of healthy behaviors.

Embracing this affirmation daily contributes to strengthening the inner belief that a healthy lifestyle is a natural part of everyday life. It highlights the importance of daily choices, such as choosing healthy meals and exercising regularly, in shaping overall health status.

Additionally, this affirmation may inspire seeking new ways to improve health, such as trying new forms of physical activity or experimenting with various, healthy recipes. In this way, "I care for my health every day" becomes not just a declaration but also a motivating guide to daily health care, which can lead to long-term, positive lifestyle changes.

Chapter 6 — Creating a Mental Image

Visualization — Your Personal Success Cinema

When affirmations become part of the daily routine, they pave the way for personal development. They can be likened to the seeds of dreams that we sow in our consciousness. To accelerate their growth, visualization proves to be an effective tool. The combination of affirmations and visualization acts as an amplifier, helping to achieve the desired state of affairs more quickly. Together, these two techniques form a powerful tool that can significantly speed up the process of achieving personal aspirations, dreams, and goals, acting as a booster for the realization of plans.

Visualization is the process of creating mental images of success, comparable to directing a film where dreams and goals are the main actors. Imagining the achievement of the goals of affirmations activates processes in the brain similar to those experienced during actual events. The brain does not always distinguish between imaginations and real experiences, making visualization an effective tool.

The visualization process begins with finding a comfortable place and adopting a relaxing posture. Closing your eyes and focusing on deep breathing helps achieve a state of inner peace. Next, one should concentrate on the affirmation, stating it mentally or aloud, and begin crafting the vision.

Visualization should be detailed, including colors, sounds, the presence of other people, and the emotions accompanying the achievement of the goal. Emotions are a key element, as they give visualization its power. Experiencing positive feelings during visualization, such as joy or pride, strengthens the belief in the achievability of goals.

A variety of visualization scenarios is recommended, yet each visualization should be consistent with the affirmation. Imagining success in various aspects helps reinforce the pursuit of the goal.

Visualization is not merely daydreaming, but a tool that prepares for action. Regular practice allows for the subconscious direction of actions towards achieving goals and noticing new opportunities.

It is said that visualization is like downloading the future into the present. Creating mental images in which goals have already been achieved gives strength, motivation, and confidence regarding the realization of intended plans.

I encourage you to frequently create mental scenarios of success, full of clarity, color, and emotion. Each visualization session is a step closer to achieving your dreams. Affirmations lay the foundation, while visualization is the brick in building the house of fulfilled intentions.

Sensory Experiences

Engaging the full spectrum of sensory perception in the process of creating mental images makes an affirmation take on a deeper dimension of reality and convincing power.

When we construct a given scene in our imagination, we do not limit ourselves to merely "seeing" it in our consciousness but also perceive sounds, sense aromas, experience the variety of touch, and even taste elements of our mental projection. This comprehensive engagement of the senses makes the imagination more intense and convincing, which consequently has a significant impact on our subconscious.

Our subconscious is not very effective at distinguishing fiction from reality, hence intense, multisensory mental creations can induce emotions and physiological responses similar to those we experience during real events.

When our brain receives these detailed and sensory-rich projections, it activates the same areas responsible for processing real experiences. For example, imagining the taste of our favorite dish can actually induce salivation.

Such deep engagement of the senses in the visualization process is crucial as it strengthens the learning and adaptation process of the brain. It aids in embedding positive beliefs and goals in our subconscious, which can be a catalyst for changing attitudes, modifying behaviors, and even contributing to the realization of specific aspirations.

For this reason, in the process of affirmation and visualization creation, emphasis is placed on creating scenarios that are as realistic and full as possible, engaging the entire palette of senses. This allows us to "experience" our aspirations and dreams in a safe, mental environment, which can effectively influence our motivation and actions in the real world.

Emotional Engagement

It is feelings that give affirmations depth and dynamics. Emotions such as joy, gratitude, or love can transform the routine, automatic repetition of affirmations into a powerful and meaningful experience. When affirmations are imbued with positive feelings, they are easier to accept and believe in their authenticity.

The subconscious, being the key recipient of affirmations, is particularly susceptible to emotional influences. Feelings act as a catalyst for the messages we wish to implement in our psyche. Affirmations enriched with intense positive emotions are more quickly and effectively accepted by the subconscious. This is because the subconscious better "decodes" the language of emotions than the language of logic.

The importance of emotional engagement in the affirmation process cannot be overstated. Feelings give affirmations their power of message, making them more suggestive. Moreover, emotions help root affirmations in our memory. Evoking positive emotional states while reciting affirmations increases the likelihood that our mind will return to them, which can result in positive changes in our behaviors and attitudes.

Emotional engagement in the affirmation process is also a way to increase our overall well-being. Positive feelings generated during affirmations can improve our moods and mental condition, which translates into better mental and physical health. This is particularly important in the context of long-term affirmation practice, where regular evocation of positive emotions can have a lasting and beneficial impact on our lives.

Below, I will give you an example of visualization and you will see how focusing on all senses — sound, smell, sight, and touch, can help create a deep and realistic scenery of your goal. Let's assume you want to buy a house with a charming garden. See, it will work like a magical mirror, allowing you to transport yourself to that magical place in your mind.

Relax, close your eyes, and focus on calm, deep breathing. Let each inhalation and exhalation bring you closer to that fairy-tale space.

Imagine standing in front of a beautiful, wooden house, woven into a picturesque landscape. Its walls are painted a warm, soothing color, and the roof is covered with dark shingles that shimmer in the sunlight. In front of the house stretches a charming garden, full of blooming flowers and lush green bushes.

Take a step forward and feel the softness of freshly cut grass under your feet. Its scent mixes with the delicate aroma of flowers, creating a soothing symphony of fragrances. You hear the gentle singing of birds, joyfully greeting the new day, their melodies bringing a sense of peace and harmony.

Continue down the path, laid with colorful stones, leading through this enchanted garden. Feel the sun gently warming your face and shoulders, and its rays filtering through the leaves of an apple tree, creating a dance of lights and shadows on the ground.

Reach a charming bench placed in the shade of a tree. Sit on it and feel the wood, warmed by the sun, pleasantly heating your body. Allow yourself a moment of rest, gazing into the expanse of the garden that is now yours. Every corner, every plant, is part of your new, wonderful world.

Now, in this tranquil place, feel the fullness of happiness and fulfillment. This is your garden, your home — a place that reflects your dreams and aspirations. Embrace this thought, feel it with all your heart.

When you're ready, slowly return to reality. Take a few deep breaths and gradually open your eyes, keeping the image of your dream home and garden in your heart. Remember, this visualization is a powerful tool that helps you move closer to fulfilling your dreams.

Frequency and Repetition

Cyclicality, the regular repetition of certain activities at fixed intervals, plays a crucial role in our lives, influencing how our brain and subconscious process and accept new information. This phenomenon is not only exploited in marketing but also holds fundamental importance in the process of affirmations.

Let's start with an everyday example. When we see the same advertisement broadcast multiple times on television or repeated posters on the streets, it's not a coincidence.

This is a deliberate marketing action, based on the principle of cyclicality. These advertisements often evoke emotions in us—both positive and negative. Marketing psychology leverages this knowledge to compel us to remember the product and, consequently, to purchase it. One might wonder why we choose a certain product in a store. Often, it's the result of being repeatedly exposed to a specific advertisement that has lodged itself in our subconscious.

Research in psychology and neurology confirms that the regular repetition of actions leads to the creation and strengthening of neural pathways in the brain. This process, known as neuroplasticity, which I've already mentioned, shows that our brain adapts and changes in response to repeated experiences. Therefore, regularly repeating affirmations helps in rooting new, positive beliefs, replacing old, negative thought patterns.

For instance, if you regularly repeat the affirmation "I am strong and capable of overcoming challenges," your subconscious begins to absorb this as truth. As you continue repeating, your actions and reactions start to reflect this belief.

The last stage in the process of affirmation is "letting go of control" and "trusting the subconscious." After a long period of regular repetition of affirmations, we begin to surrender to the natural flow of our thoughts and actions. This no longer requires conscious effort, as the affirmations become part of our subconscious thoughts and behaviors. Then, we may notice that the changes we wanted to implement begin to occur automatically.

By incorporating this knowledge into our daily lives, we can consciously shape our thoughts, beliefs, and behaviors, utilizing the power of cyclicality and regularity.

Affirmations are not just momentary declarations but tools that, combined with regular repetition, can lead to significant, positive changes in our lives.

Creating Personalized Affirmations

The process of creating personalized affirmations begins with thorough introspection to understand individual aspirations, needs, and the current emotional state.

The first step is to identify and accept the current emotions, which may include melancholy, tension, euphoria, chronic stress, anxieties, or other states. At this point, if you feel that working on yourself alone is not enough, do not hesitate to seek help from a behavioral therapy specialist or psychologist. Asking for support is an important step.

Behavioral therapy specialists focus mainly on modifying behaviors, using techniques such as cognitive-behavioral therapy (CBT) and other behavioral methods. Their work often concentrates on specific issues, such as eating disorders, addictions, anxieties, or behavioral disorders.

Psychologists deal with more complex mental issues, such as deeply rooted emotional problems, personality disorders, or chronic mental issues.

Recording feelings in an emotional diary often facilitates the regular recognition of dominant states and discovering their potential causes.

Next, you should consider what might be the source of these emotions. Understanding the causes of emotional states is the cornerstone of creating effective affirmations. For example, in the case of professional stress, an appropriate affirmation might be: "I possess the skills and will successfully overcome professional challenges," and in the face of feeling isolated: "I am a person of value and am open to forming new relationships."

It's crucial that the affirmations created are realistic and resonate with individual values and goals. General affirmations may not have as strong an impact as those carefully tailored to personal experiences. Affirmations should be realistic and achievable, reflecting a positive image of oneself and aspirations.

Regular repetition of affirmations is key to their effectiveness. Incorporating them into your daily routine, whether in the morning, evening, or throughout the day when you need them, helps internalize positive beliefs and transform negative thinking into a more productive and positive outlook.

Chapter 7 — Diversity of Affirmation Forms

Enriching Daily Routine

Using various forms of repeating affirmations can be an effective way to strengthen their impact and diversify your daily routine.

Here are some creative ideas:

— **Speaking Aloud** — Start your day by loudly repeating affirmations during morning activities, such as brushing your teeth or preparing breakfast. This is not only a great way to set a positive tone for the entire day but also to integrate affirmations into your routine. For example, you might repeat, "Today is my day, full of successes and positive experiences!"

— **Writing** — Maintain an affirmation journal. Write different affirmations daily, creating a personal collection of positive thoughts. You can also create colorful sticky notes with affirmations and place them in areas you frequently visit, like your desk, refrigerator, or mirror. This not only facilitates reminding yourself of the affirmations but also visually enriches your environment.

— **Thinking** — Practice affirmations in your thoughts during spare moments, such as while riding the bus or waiting in line. This is a good way to mentally refresh and focus on positive thoughts. For instance, concentrate on an affirmation like, "Every moment is an opportunity for growth and learning."

— **Singing** — If you enjoy singing, try transforming your affirmations into short melodies. You can sing them in the shower or on your way to work. This not only reinforces the affirmations but also makes them a joyful part of your day. For example, "I am strong, I am wise, every day is my triumph!"

— **Creative Visualizations** — Imagine yourself achieving the goals of your affirmations. This can be a powerful tool to increase your motivation and self-belief. Visualize yourself succeeding at work, being healthy, or surrounded by positive relationships.

— **Drawing or Painting Affirmations** — If you like drawing or painting, try expressing your affirmations through art. You could, for example, create a poster with an affirmation at the center, adorned with patterns, colors, and symbols that mean something to you. This visual representation of the affirmation not only strengthens its message but also serves as a beautiful decoration, reminding you of your goals and positive intentions every day. You can also create new artworks related to different affirmations, experimenting with colors and techniques, making the process both creative and therapeutic.

To maintain the cyclicality and regularity of using affirmations, it's important to choose methods that best fit your lifestyle and personality. Experiment with different approaches and see which ones you resonate with the most.

Regular use of affirmations can bring significant benefits to your well-being and positive outlook on life, as well as the realization of desires. Remember, each method has its unique benefits and can affect your awareness and emotions differently. Finding the right balance and combination of methods is key to effectively using affirmations in everyday life.

Affirmation Examples — Your Source of Inspiration

In this section, I present you with carefully selected affirmation examples, serving as a source of inspiration and motivation. They are general in nature and not tailored to the specific needs or situations of readers.

Their main task is to inspire the creation of your own, unique affirmations that fully respond to your individual desires, dreams, and goals.

I encourage you to explore these contents with an open mind and heart. You can adapt, modify, or even create entirely new ones, reflecting your personal aspirations.

Morning Affirmations

- *I am grateful for another beautiful day.*

- *My thoughts are filled with positive energy and optimism.*

- *Each new breath fills me with peace and strength.*

- *I am the creator of my own happiness and well-being.*

- *Today, I make wise decisions and choices.*

- *I am open to new experiences and learning.*

• *My self-confidence grows with every moment.*

• *I am grateful for the love I receive and give.*

• *I possess peace and harmony, which guide me throughout the day.*

• *Every action brings me closer to my dreams.*

• *Patience and perseverance are my strengths.*

• *Today, I develop my creativity and innovation.*

• *I am surrounded by positive people and energy.*

• *Today is full of promises and opportunities.*

• *Today brings joy and fulfillment.*

Evening Affirmations

• *I am thankful for all of today's experiences.*

• *The evening brings me peace and renewal.*

• *I am thankful for the pleasant moments and joy I experienced today.*

• *Every breath provides me with deep relaxation and peace.*

• *With gratitude, I prepare for a restful sleep.*

• *I am thankful for the health, strength, and abundance in my life.*

- *I feel gratitude for the love and support around me.*

- *My mind is calm, and my heart is filled with love.*

- *I am thankful for today's inspirations and ideas.*

- *I rest knowing that each new day is full of possibilities.*

- *With each breath, I feel peace and harmony growing within me.*

- *I am grateful for my safe home and the warmth of my family.*

- *I am thankful for the inner strength I displayed today.*

- *I enter a state of deep relaxation, preparing for peaceful sleep.*

- *With gratitude and joy, I end this day, looking forward to tomorrow full of new experiences.*

Affirmations Supporting Abundance and Financial Opportunities

- *I am thankful for the financial abundance flowing into my life.*

- *I am a magnet for wealth and prosperity.*

- *My actions lead me to continuous financial growth.*

- *I feel gratitude for financial stability and security.*

- *Each day brings new opportunities to increase my prosperity.*

- *I am open to new sources of income and wealth.*

- *My mind is filled with positive thoughts about money and abundance.*

- *I believe in my ability to achieve financial freedom.*

- *I am thankful for the universe's generosity that continuously supports me.*

- *With each day, I become more aware of my financial possibilities.*

- *I am thankful for every influx of money into my life.*

- *My financial decisions are wise and considered.*

- *Everything I do contributes to my wealth.*

- *I am thankful for harmony and balance in my finances.*

- *I am grateful for the constant growth of my assets.*

Affirmations Supporting Physical Health Aspects

- *I feel strong and full of energy every day.*

- *My body becomes healthier and more vital with each day.*

- *I appreciate and respect my body for all it does for me.*

- *Every meal and physical activity enhances my health.*

- *I am grateful for improving health and vitality.*

- *My body becomes stronger and healthier every day.*

- *I follow my body's guidance towards health.*

- *I feel how my body gratefully responds to healthy habits.*

- *Each new day brings me health and vitality.*

- *I am open to new ways of caring for my health.*

- *With gratitude, I receive all the health benefits that come my way.*

- *My mind and body are in perfect harmony.*

- *I feel relaxed and at peace, contributing to my health.*

- *Every cell in my body is filled with energy and health.*

- *I am grateful for my body's natural healing ability.*

Affirmations Supporting Professional Career

- *Every day, I develop my skills and gain new knowledge that leads me to success.*

- *I am a valuable employee, and my work is appreciated.*

- *My career is characterized by continuous growth and achieving set goals.*

- *I encounter new, exciting professional opportunities.*

- *I have the strength and determination to achieve greater successes.*

- *My contribution to work brings visible and positive results.*

- *I am a leader who inspires others and contributes to the company's growth.*

- *I have the confidence and skills needed for advancement.*

- *Every day at work brings new, positive challenges and satisfaction.*

- *I am open to new ideas and innovations that bring success.*

- *My communication abilities are key to my professional achievements.*

- *The work I do is a source of joy and satisfaction for me.*

- *My professional relationships are based on mutual respect and cooperation.*

- *Every day, I see progress in my career and pursuit of goals.*

- *I am grateful for all my achievements so far and excitedly await new ones.*

- *I am open to love and give love unconditionally.*

- *I have healthy and loving relationships with the people around me.*

- *Every day, I attract positive and supportive relationships into my life.*

- *I feel deep gratitude for the love I receive and express.*

- *I am full of empathy, understanding, and warmth for others.*

- *My strength is the ability to build lasting and healthy relationships.*

- *Every new acquaintance is an opportunity to enrich my life.*

- *I am a valuable partner, friend, and family member.*

- *Harmony, respect, and happiness prevail in my relationships.*

- *Every conversation with loved ones enriches our mutual bond and understanding.*

- *I am a source of positive energy for the people in my environment.*

- *I love and am loved for who I am.*

- *I have the courage to be authentic in my relationships.*

- *My heart is open to receiving and giving love.*

- *I am thankful for all the wonderful relationships in my life.*

Affirmations Supporting Daily Well-being and Self-esteem

- *Every day, I accept myself with all strengths and weaknesses, feeling completely comfortable in my skin.*

- *Every day, I feel confident and full of positive energy.*

- *I fully and lovingly accept myself.*

- *My inner self is full of peace and harmony.*

- *Every day, I recognize my value and uniqueness.*

- *I am strong, capable, and competent.*

- *Self-trust guides me through life.*

- *Every day, I grow stronger and develop my skills.*

- *I am proud of my achievements, big and small.*

- *Every day, I direct my thoughts towards reinforcing my self-esteem and well-being.*

- *I believe in my abilities and talent.*

- *I am a valuable person who makes a positive contribution to the world.*

- *I have the power to influence my life and make positive changes.*

- *My self-esteem is high because I know my worth.*

- *I thank myself for perseverance, love, and care I show towards myself.*

Affirmations Supporting Spiritual Development and Self-awareness

- *Every day, I deepen my understanding of my inner self and my spiritual path.*

- *I am open to profound spiritual experiences and personal growth.*

- *With each day, my intuition becomes stronger and more precise.*

- *I feel a deep inner peace stemming from understanding my true self.*

- *I consciously connect with the universal energy of love and light.*

- *I am grateful for every lesson that leads me to spiritual growth.*

- *Each day brings me greater inner harmony and balance.*

• *Meditation and reflection are key elements of my spiritual development.*

• *I trust the process of life and know I am on the right spiritual path.*

• *I accept and love myself, which is the foundation of my spiritual journey.*

• *I am connected to the greater whole and feel this unity every day.*

• *My spiritual development brings me deep understanding of myself and the world.*

• *Every day, I find deeper self-understanding and awareness of the world around me.*

• *I embrace peace and love as fundamental values of my life.*

• *I am infinitely open to all the blessings the universe brings me.*

Chapter 8 — Resources and Inspirations

Success Stories

The tales of my students who have achieved significant personal development through their work with affirmations and meditation.

"I found Katarzyna's course in 2020, searching for help in the despair of my gray, lonely days. My name is Aneta. My life turned upside down when my long-term partner decided to leave. That was the moment I felt my self-esteem drop below zero. I felt lonely, desperate, invisible, and unattractive in my own eyes.

I started with skepticism. Affirmations? How could they possibly help? But deep inside, a spark of hope flickered that maybe this was a way to reclaim myself.

After a brief therapy, Katarzyna introduced me to the world of affirmations. It was hard at first. Looking in the mirror and saying, 'I am strong, I am beautiful, I am enough' — sounded like a lie. But with each day, it became easier. I repeated those words, first in a whisper, then louder and louder. And I began to believe them.

It wasn't an easy process. There were days when tears flooded my face, when I doubted the sense of all these affirmations. But the instructor was my guide, my support. She taught me that the road to regaining self-belief is a marathon, not a sprint.

Then, about half a year later, something changed. I began to notice how people reacted to my changed attitude. I became more open, more confident. And one day, in a café where I usually sat alone with a book, someone approached me. It was Krzysztof. He smiled at me and asked if he could join. We talked for hours. He was different from anyone I had met before. Honest, full of empathy, interested in me just as I am.

Now, looking back, I see how much I've changed thanks to affirmations and learning meditation. I understood that my worth does not depend on whether I am in a relationship or not. I found peace within myself, and then love came. This story is a reminder to me that even in the darkest moments, there is light; you just have to believe that you can find it. Thanks to Katarzyna and her help, I not only regained faith in myself but also opened up to a new chapter in my life.

Aneta Warowska"

"I fell out of life and into a wheelchair after a car accident when I was 40. For a year, with the help of a psychologist, I tried to understand and accept my new reality. But I still felt something was missing, something that would bring me back to the life I so desperately wanted.

One day, browsing the Internet, I stumbled upon the course. Pointless — I thought then — How could simple techniques and meditation exercises help someone in my situation?

To this day, I don't know why I tried.

The course was a challenge, I long fought with myself.

Over time, it taught me how important it is to accept myself and my situation, how valuable it is to appreciate the little things. I began each day with affirmations that initially seemed foreign and unbelievable. 'I am strong. I am valuable. My life has meaning.' These words became my daily mantra.

With each day, I felt a growing strength and determination not to give up. Small but significant changes began to happen. I wanted to talk more with people, to open up to new experiences. Friends and family noticed a change in my attitude. I became more positive, less focused on my limitations, and more on possibilities.

The biggest turnaround for me was deciding to go to a local meeting for people with disabilities. There, I met a group of incredible people who, like me, faced their own challenges. Finding this community gave me a sense of belonging and understanding.

Now, looking back, I see how much the course changed my life. It taught me that my value does not depend on my physical limitations. It taught me that even in the darkest moments, hope can be found. Not only did I accept myself and my situation, but I also found a new meaning and joy in life.

Thank you.

Artur Jagielski"

"My name is Ola, I am 20 years old, and my life has never been easy. I grew up in a home where alcohol was an everyday occurrence, and then in a foster family. I experienced pain and suffering, both

mentally and physically. These difficult experiences made me scared of life, struggling with anxiety, and even attempting to find escape in drugs and alcohol.

When it seemed like there was no hope for me, my sister helped me find a way out. She directed me to specialized treatment, which helped me battle the demons of the past for two years. I slowly started returning to normal life, but still, sometimes, that overwhelming sense of hopelessness and paralyzing anxiety would return.

That's when Beata brought me to the therapy led by the lady. It was different from anything I had experienced before. It taught me how important it is to accept oneself, understand one's emotions, and deal with them in a healthy way. Slowly but surely, I started applying the tools and techniques she showed me. Affirmations became my daily ritual, giving me strength and courage to face each new day.

Over time, I noticed that I started to view the world differently. Less fear, more hope. I began engaging in various activities, finding joy in little things. It was a completely new beginning for me.

Now, looking back, I see how much I've changed thanks to therapy. I realized that my past experiences do not define me as a person. I learned that I can reshape my life anew, with hope and courage. Thanks to the support of the lady and this therapy, I found a strength in me I never thought I possessed. It was a journey full of challenges, but also incredibly rewarding. Thanks to it, I can now face the future stronger than ever before.

Ola Wojnowska"

Affirmation Journal

Dear Reader,

I invite you to the challenge of using the Affirmation Journal for the next month.

Invest in a notebook specifically designated for affirmation practices and make entries daily, following the suggested template. Not only should you transcribe the quote of the day and the affirmation of the day, but most importantly, record your own affirmations, analyze and assess your emotions and feelings.

Why is it worthwhile? Because this tool can significantly impact your way of thinking, self-esteem, and overall approach to life. For the next 28 days, you will have the opportunity to work on yourself, your emotions, and your thinking.

- *Daily practice will allow you to focus on the positive aspects of life and yourself.*

- *You will boost your self-esteem and sense of self-worth through systematic application of the practices contained here.*

- *You will learn how to cope with stress and anxiety through various techniques.*

- *Use this tool to focus on your goals and dreams and strive to achieve them.*

In the journal, you will find not only daily tips but also tasks, inspiring quotes, space for reflection, and thanksgiving. Every day is a new opportunity to strengthen yourself.

I encourage you to take up this challenge.

Spend a few minutes each day working with the journal. Let these practices accompany you throughout the day; you can repeat them or write them down. Use one for the entire week or adjust to your needs. The important thing is to develop the habit of daily exercises.

You may be surprised at how great a change can be brought about by their regular application and mindful reflections.

Begin this journey with me and discover how you can strengthen your life from the inside.

I wish you an inspiring journey full of discoveries!

Week One: Discovering the Power of Affirmations

Day 1: Beginning the Journey

Quote of the Day: *"The beginning is the most important part of the work." — Plato*

Daily Affirmation: *"Today, I embark on my journey with affirmations, opening myself to new possibilities."*

Your Affirmation:

Small Task of the Day: *Write down three goals you want to achieve using affirmations.*

Rate your emotions and feelings today (Scale 0—5):

Calmness —

Energy —

Satisfaction —

Evening Summary: *How did today's affirmation affect your thoughts and actions?*

Day 2: Understanding Affirmations

Quote of the Day: *"Everything that is repeated is strengthened." — Unknown Author*

Daily Affirmation: *"Today, I focus on understanding the power of affirmations in my life."*

Your Affirmation:

Small Task of the Day: *Write down the emotions evoked by today's affirmation.*

Rate your emotions and feelings today (Scale 0—5):

Acceptance —

Motivation —

Understanding —

Evening Summary: *What new understanding of affirmations did you gain today?*

Day 3: Practicing Affirmations

Quote of the Day: *"Practice makes perfect." — Unknown Author*

Daily Affirmation: *"From today, I consistently practice affirmations to see their effects."*

Your Affirmation:

Small Task of the Day: *Choose one affirmation and repeat it throughout the day in different situations. You can write it down if you prefer.*

Rate your emotions and feelings today (Scale 0—5):

Determination —

Consistency —

Optimism —

Evening Summary: *What changes have you noticed in your thinking and behavior?*

Day 4: Discovering the Impact of Affirmations

Quote of the Day: *"Thoughts shape words, words shape actions." — Unknown Author*

Daily Affirmation: *"Every affirmation of mine positively influences my daily life."*

Your Affirmation:

Small Task of the Day: *Observe how your affirmations affect your decisions and actions throughout the day. Note this down.*

Rate your emotions and feelings today (Scale 0—5):

Awareness —

Impact —

Control —

Evening Summary: *What positive changes have you noticed due to affirmations?*

Day 5: Strengthening Positive Thinking

Quote of the Day: *"Positive thinking attracts positive events." — Unknown Author*

Daily Affirmation: *"Today, I focus on the positive aspect of every situation."*

Your Affirmation:

Small Task of the Day: *Find a positive aspect in every difficult situation you encounter today. Note it down.*

Rate your emotions and feelings today (Scale 0—5):

Satisfaction —

Gratitude —

Positivism —

Evening Summary: *How has your perception of challenges changed due to positive thinking?*

Day 6: Affirmations and Self-Acceptance

Quote of the Day: *"Self-acceptance is the first step to inner harmony." — Unknown Author*

Daily Affirmation: *"I completely accept and love myself as I am."*

Your Affirmation:

Small Task of the Day: *Spend a few moments thinking about your strengths and accept your weaknesses. Describe your strengths.*

Rate your emotions and feelings today (Scale 0—5):

Self-confidence — S

elf-acceptance —

Self-belief —

Evening Summary: *In which areas did you feel greater self-acceptance today?*

Day 7: Week in Review

Quote of the Day: *"Reflection is the key to learning." — Unknown Author*

Daily Affirmation: *"I summarize my weekly journey with affirmations, drawing lessons and inspiration from it."*

Your Affirmation:

Small Task of the Day: *Make a summary of the week, write down what you have learned and the changes you have noticed.*

Rate your emotions and feelings today (Scale 0—5):

Reflection —

Understanding —

Gratitude —

Evening Summary: What are your main conclusions from this week of affirmations?

Week Two: Building Inner Strength

Day 8: Recognizing Inner Strength

Quote of the Day: *"Strength does not come from physical capacity. It comes from an indomitable will." — Mahatma Gandhi*

Daily Affirmation: *"Every day, I discover and strengthen my inner strength."*

Your Affirmation:

Small Task of the Day: *Identify and write down a moment when you showed inner strength.*

Rate your emotions and feelings today (Scale 0—5):

Resilience —

Self-control —

Confidence —

Evening Summary: *How did today's actions reflect your inner strength?*

Day 9: Overcoming Obstacles

Quote of the Day: *"Obstacles don't have to stop you. If you run into a wall, don't turn around and give up. Figure out how to climb it." — Michael Jordan*

Daily Affirmation: *"Obstacles are an opportunity for growth and learning for me."*

Your Affirmation:

Small Task of the Day: *Reflect on an obstacle you have recently overcome and what it has given you. Note your thoughts.*

Rate your emotions and feelings today (Scale 0—5):

Perseverance —

Resilience —

Adaptability —

Evening Summary: *How did today's affirmation help you in approaching challenges?*

Day 10: Courage in Action

Quote of the Day: *"Courage doesn't always roar. Sometimes courage is the quiet voice at the end of the day saying, 'I will try again tomorrow.'" — Mary Anne Radmacher*

Daily Affirmation: *"Today, I act with courage, even if it means stepping out of my comfort zone."*

Your Affirmation:

Small Task of the Day: *Do something you would not usually dare to do. Describe your success.*

Rate your emotions and feelings today (Scale 0—5):

Courage —

Determination —

Enthusiasm —

Evening Summary: *In what actions did you demonstrate courage today?*

Day 11: Strengthening Self-Esteem

Quote of the Day: *"Believe in yourself, respect your dreams, trust yourself." — Norman Vincent Peale*

Daily Affirmation: *"I appreciate myself and believe in my abilities."*

Your Affirmation:

Small Task of the Day: *Write down three things you value most about yourself.*

Rate your emotions and feelings today (Scale 0—5):

Self-acceptance —

Well-being —

Pride —

Evening Summary: *What aspects of yourself did you particularly appreciate today?*

Day 12: Developing Self-Discipline

Quote of the Day: *"Self-discipline begins with the mastery of your thoughts. If you don't control them, you don't control anything." — Napoleon Hill*

Daily Affirmation: *"Every day, I develop my self-discipline and focus."*

Your Affirmation:

Small Task of the Day: *Set a small goal and achieve it today without delay. Note it down.*

Rate your emotions and feelings today (Scale 0—5):

Focus —

Self-control —

Discipline —

Evening Summary: *How did you manage to maintain discipline in pursuing your goal today?*

Day 13: Finding Inner Balance

Quote of the Day: *"Balance is not something you find, it's something you create." — Jana Kingsford*

Daily Affirmation: *"Today, I strive for inner balance and peace."*

Your Affirmation:

Small Task of the Day: *Perform a short meditation or relaxation exercise. Note your feelings.*

Rate your emotions and feelings today (Scale 0—5):

Calm —

Harmony —

Balance —

Evening Summary: *What steps did you take today towards achieving inner balance?*

Day 14: Summary and Reflection

Quote of the Day: *"The best learning comes from introspection and reflecting on one's own experiences." — Unknown Author*

Daily Affirmation: *"I summarize my experiences from the past week, drawing strength and motivation from them."*

Your Affirmation:

Small Task of the Day: *Look back on the past week and consider the progress you have made in building inner strength. Make notes.*

Rate your emotions and feelings today (Scale 0—5):

Motivation —

Growth —

Insight —

Evening Summary: *What are your main conclusions from this week, and how do you plan to use these lessons in the future?*

Week Three: Developing Gratitude

Day 15: Introduction to Gratitude

Quote of the Day: *"Gratitude turns what we have into enough."* — Melody Beattie

Daily Affirmation: *"Today, I notice and appreciate the good around me."*

Your Affirmation:

Small Task of the Day: *Write down three things you are grateful for today.*

Rate your emotions and feelings today (Scale 0—5):

Calm —

Positive Attitude —

Gratitude —

Evening Summary: *What moments today aroused the most gratitude in you?*

Day 16: Appreciating the Little Things

Quote of the Day: *"The most beautiful things in life are not seen nor touched, but are felt in the heart."* — Helen Keller

Daily Affirmation: *"Every day, I find beauty and value in the small things."*

Your Affirmation:

Small Task of the Day: *Pay attention to the day's small pleasures and note them down.*

Rate your emotions and feelings today (Scale 0—5):

Mindfulness —

Satisfaction —

Gratitude —

Evening Summary: *What small things brought you joy today?*

Day 17: Gratitude for Relationships and Connections

Quote of the Day: *"To be loved is something. To love and be loved is everything." — T. Tolis*

Daily Affirmation: *"I am grateful for the people in my life and their impact on me."*

Your Affirmation:

Small Task of the Day: *Send a message of thanks to someone who recently had a positive impact on you. Describe your feelings.*

Rate your emotions and feelings today (Scale 0—5):

Love —

Connection —

Empathy —

Evening Summary: *How did you express gratitude to others today?*

Day 18: Reflecting on the Past

Quote of the Day: *"Do not dwell in the past, do not dream of the future, concentrate the mind on the present moment." — Buddha*

Daily Affirmation: *"I draw lessons and gratitude from my past experiences."*

Your Affirmation:

Small Task of the Day: *Reflect on a challenging experience from the past and find a reason for gratitude. Make notes.*

Rate your emotions and feelings today (Scale 0—5):

Growth —

Gratitude —

Reasoning —

Evening Summary: *How have past experiences enriched your life?*

Day 19: Gratitude for Challenges

Quote of the Day: *"Challenges make life interesting, overcoming them makes life meaningful." — Joshua J. Marine*

Daily Affirmation: *"In every challenge, I see an opportunity for growth, and I am grateful for it."*

Your Affirmation:

Small Task of the Day: *Take on a small challenge today and note how it made you feel.*

Rate your emotions and feelings today (Scale 0—5):

Strength —

Gratitude —

Challenge —

Evening Summary: *What lessons and values did you take from today's challenges?*

Day 20: Mindfully Appreciating Life

Quote of the Day: *"Life is a gift, and gratitude for it transforms every moment into a miracle." — Unknown Author*

Daily Affirmation: *"Every day, I mindfully appreciate the gift of life."*

Your Affirmation:

Small Task of the Day: *Spend a moment appreciating life through mindful breathing or meditation. Note your feelings.*

Rate your emotions and feelings today (Scale 0—5):

Mindfulness —

Calm —

Gratitude —

Evening Summary: *How did you celebrate and appreciate life today?*

Day 21: Week of Gratitude Summary

Quote of the Day: *"Reflection is a way to find beauty in every past."* — *Unknown Author*

Daily Affirmation: *"I reflect on the past week, drawing from it gratitude and wisdom."*

Your Affirmation:

Small Task of the Day: *Write a summary of this week, focusing on moments of gratitude.*

Rate your emotions and feelings today (Scale 0—5):

Insight —

Satisfaction —

Gratitude —

Evening Summary: *What are your main takeaways from analyzing a week of developing gratitude?*

Week Four: Finding Joy in Everyday Life

Day 22: Mindfulness of Joyful Moments

Quote of the Day: *"Joy does not reside in things; it dwells within us."* — *Richard Wagner*

Daily Affirmation: *"Today, I notice and relish every moment of joy."*

Your Affirmation:

Small Task of the Day: *Pay attention to the moments that bring you joy today, even the smallest ones. Note them down.*

Rate your emotions and feelings today (Scale 0—5):

Joy —

Satisfaction —

Mindfulness —

Evening Summary: Which moments brought you the most joy today?

Day 23: Appreciating Simple Pleasures

Quote of the Day: "Simple pleasures are the last healthy refuge in a complex world." — Oscar Wilde

Daily Affirmation: "In the simplicity of everyday life, I find true joy."

Your Affirmation:

Small Task of the Day: Find joy in a simple daily activity and celebrate it. Note your feelings.

Rate your emotions and feelings today (Scale 0—5):

Satisfaction —

Calm —

Gratitude —

Evening Summary: What simple pleasures brought you joy today?

Day 24: Joy in Interacting with Others

Quote of the Day: *"Share your spark of joy with others, and it becomes a flame." — Unknown Author*

Daily Affirmation: *"My interactions with others are a source of mutual joy."*

Your Affirmation:

Small Task of the Day: *Initiate a conversation or activity that brings joy to you and others. Describe your feelings.*

Rate your emotions and feelings today (Scale 0—5):

Cooperation —

Empathy —

Joy —

Evening Summary: *How did interactions with others affect your sense of joy?*

Day 25: Finding Joy in Life's Lessons

Quote of the Day: *"Life isn't about avoiding the storms, but about learning to dance in the rain." — Vivian Greene*

Daily Affirmation: *"Every life experience is an opportunity to find joy."*

Your Affirmation:

Small Task of the Day: *Reflect on a recent challenge and find its source of joy. Describe it.*

Rate your emotions and feelings today (Scale 0—5):

Optimism —

Strength —

Joy —

Evening Summary: *What life lessons brought you joy today?*

Day 26: Celebrating Achievements

Quote of the Day: *"Every small achievement is a step towards joy."* — *Unknown Author*

Daily Affirmation: *"Today, I celebrate my achievements, big and small."*

Your Affirmation:

Small Task of the Day: *Make a list of your recent achievements and celebrate them.*

Rate your emotions and feelings today (Scale 0—5):

Pride —

Satisfaction —

Joy —

Evening Summary: *Which achievements brought you joy today?*

Day 27: Joy in Nature

Quote of the Day: *"Nature is a painting for our eyes." — Henry David Thoreau*

Daily Affirmation: *"I find joy in the beauty and peace of nature."*

Your Affirmation:

Small Task of the Day: *Spend time outdoors, observing and enjoying nature. Describe your feelings.*

Rate your emotions and feelings today (Scale 0—5):

Calm —

Satisfaction —

Gratitude —

Evening Summary: *How did contact with nature affect your sense of joy?*

Day 28: Week of Joy Summary

Quote of the Day: *"Reflection is the key to celebrating life." — Unknown Author*

Daily Affirmation: *"I summarize the week, rejoicing in every moment of joy."*

Your Affirmation:

Small Task of the Day: *Look back on the week and consider which moments brought you the most joy. Make notes.*

Rate your emotions and feelings today (Scale 0—5):

Insight —

Satisfaction —

Joy —

Evening Summary: *What are your main conclusions from this week of seeking joy?*

Summary

Congratulations! You have just completed a month of working with the affirmation journal. This is an incredible achievement and an important step in your personal development journey. Now, with a month of affirmation practice, meditation, and self-awareness work behind you, you have a unique opportunity to continue this beautiful journey.

Remember, personal development is a continuous process. Every day brings new opportunities for learning, growth, and self-discovery. I encourage you not to stop here. Here are some ways you can continue your adventure:

Continue Affirmation Practice: Stick with daily affirmations. You can create new affirmations that match your current goals and needs.

Regular Meditation: If meditation was part of your practice, try to maintain regularity. Meditation is a powerful tool for achieving peace of mind and a better understanding of yourself.

Self-Awareness Journal: Consider keeping a personal journal where you will continue to write down your thoughts, feelings, and experiences. It's a great way to gain a deeper understanding of yourself and your reactions to different situations.

Setting New Goals: Define new goals, both short-term and long-term. These goals can relate to your personal development, health, relationships, career, or other areas of life.

Education and Development: Look for new sources of knowledge and inspiration. Read books, participate in workshops, listen to podcasts on topics that interest you and develop you.

Support Community: Consider joining groups or communities that focus on personal development and mutual support.

Remember, every day is a new chance for growth and self-discovery. Your journey to inner peace, happiness, and fulfillment is ongoing, and every step, even the smallest, is of great significance.

I'm rooting for you and wish you luck on this wonderful path!

Bibliography

— Brown, Brené. "The Gifts of Imperfection: Let Go of Who You Think You're Supposed to Be and Embrace Who You Are." Hazelden Publishing, 2010.

— Dyer, Wayne W. "Your Erroneous Zones." Avon Books, 1976.

— Gilbert, Elizabeth. "Big Magic: Creative Living Beyond Fear." Riverhead Books, 2015.

— Jampolsky, Gerald G. "Love Is Letting Go of Fear." Celestial Arts, 1979.

— Kabat-Zinn, Jon. "Wherever You Go, There You Are: Mindfulness Meditation in Everyday Life." Hyperion, 1994.

— Peale, Norman Vincent. "The Power of Positive Thinking." Prentice Hall, 1952.

— Sincero, Jen. "You Are a Badass: How to Stop Doubting Your Greatness and Start Living an Awesome Life." Running Press, 2013.

Don't miss out!

Visit the website below and you can sign up to receive emails whenever Katarzyna Biedrzycka publishes a new book. There's no charge and no obligation.

https://books2read.com/r/B-A-RXXCB-OWRVC

BOOKS2READ

Connecting independent readers to independent writers.

Also by Katarzyna Biedrzycka

Huna
Huna - Discovering the Path to Your Silence

Mental Landscapes
Mental Landscapes - Practical Guide to Effective Meditation for Beginners
Mental Landscapes - Practical Guide to Effective Affirmations for Beginners

About the Author

Katarzyna Biedrzycka — a personal trainer, coach, author of books and publications. She conducts efficiency workshops in the field of professional and personal development, goal achievement, stress management, and improving the quality of life across its various aspects. In her work, she utilizes the knowledge and wisdom of Huna, as well as relaxation and meditation techniques, as effective tools for practicing the principles of the limitless power of the human mind, upon which our life in this reality is based.